Please renew/return this item by the last date shown.

From Area codes 01923 or 020:	From Area codes of Herts:
Renewals: 01923 471373	01438 737373
Enquiries: 01923 471333	01438 737333
Textphone: 01923 471599	01438 737599

www.hertsdirect.org/librarycatalogue

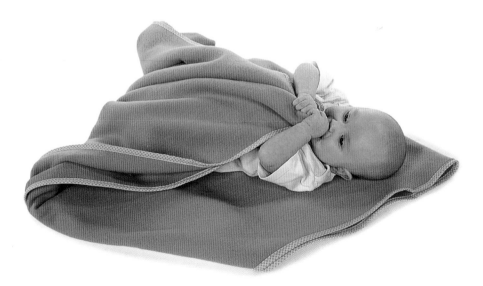

PRACTICAL parenting

Sleep

Helping your child to sleep through the night

Siobhan Stirling

hamlyn

An Hachette UK Company
www.hachette.co.uk

A Pyramid Paperback

First published in Great Britain in
2003 by Hamlyn, a division of
Octopus Publishing Group Ltd
2–4 Heron Quays, London E14 4JP
www.octopusbooks.co.uk
www.octopusbooksusa.com

This edition published in 2009

Distributed in the U.S. and Canada
by Octopus Books USA:
c/o Hachette Book Group
237 Park Avenue
New York NY 10017

This material was previously
published as *Sleep*

ISBN 978-0-600-61966-6

A CIP catalogue record for this
book is available from the British
Library

Printed and bound in China

10 9 8 7 6 5 4 3 2 1

contents

Introduction

Sleep. It's probably something you take for granted, until you have children – and then it becomes an obsession.

Above *After a good night's sleep, your child will wake refreshed and ready to face the new day.*

How many times have you seen bleary-eyed parents pushing around a bright-eyed baby or toddler during late-night shopping, desperately hoping that the hum of the supermarket aisles will lull them into slumber? How often have you heard the new dad in your office recount the number of times his little cherub had him out of bed during the night?

It is perhaps not surprising that sleep can become something of a Holy Grail for new parents. Becoming a parent is an amazing and exhilarating experience, but it is also a tiring one. Pregnancy and labour can be physically and emotionally draining (for dads as well as mums!), but once your baby arrives the hard work really begins: this little person has round-the-clock demands, and it's your job to meet them.

This can be crippling if you are used to eight hours' uninterrupted sleep a night. Not only will you be getting less sleep than you are used to, but what you do get is broken. This means you are unlikely to get the balance of deep sleep and shallow 'Rapid Eye Movement' sleep you need to help you feel refreshed.

However, it's not all doom and gloom. Research suggests that 95 per cent of children, including those with severe learning disabilities, are physiologically capable of sleeping through the night by the age of 6 months, while wide-ranging evidence confirms that older children with a history of disturbed nights can also be encouraged to go to sleep in their own beds and stay there within a relatively short time. But neither babies nor older children can achieve this on their own – they need guidance from you.

This book is designed to give you the tools and confidence you need to help your child achieve your dream of sleeping all night long. It offers a variety of practical techniques for you to adopt and adapt to suit your family. While no approach can be guaranteed to be 100 per cent effective, all the strategies have been successfully used by parents across the globe. Although every child and every family is unique, there is no reason why you cannot be as successful as the thousands of parents who have paved the way before you.

Sweet dreams!

Right *Successful sleep strategies work for children of all ages.*

your newborn
and sleep

1

- The facts

- Your baby's sleep requirements

- Where will your baby sleep?

- Sleeping safely

- If it all gets too much

The facts

We've all heard the phrase 'sleeping like a baby', and it is true that young babies do appear to be able to sleep any time, any place, anywhere – sometimes! At others, they seem to be disturbed by the slightest noise, or show no inclination for sleep when you are about to drop on your feet. If your baby's sleeping patterns have you baffled, it is helpful to start by understanding how she sleeps.

There are a lot of myths about babies and sleep, and you are likely to receive plenty of conflicting advice. So here are some facts about your baby and sleep:

- It is impossible for a newborn baby to get too much sleep.
- On average, a newborn baby sleeps for 16–17 hours per day. This drops to 13–14 hours per day by the time she is 6 months old. Your baby may sleep more or less than this.
- A newborn does not know the difference between night and day. Moreover, before she is born your baby may establish a pattern of waking up as you go to bed. The extra space in your abdomen as you lie down may encourage her to stretch her limbs a bit, while your inactivity means she is no longer being rocked to sleep.

Left *Breast-fed babies can appear sleepy for the first couple of days, but they come to life around day three when the milk comes through.*

- Many babies, especially those who are breastfed, seem to sleep around the clock for the first couple of days. This is because the watery pre-milk that they receive initially, called colostrum, is very thin, giving them little incentive to wake up to feed. But once the milk comes through at around day three, they come to life!

Above *Young babies wake several times during the night, but by the age of 2 months they have the ability to soothe themselves back to sleep.*

- Young babies spend proportionately more time in the shallow 'Rapid Eye Movement' phase of sleep than adults. This makes them much lighter sleepers and therefore much more easily disturbed.
- All babies wake several times a night during their 'shallow' sleep phases. The difference between a good sleeper and a disturbed sleeper is that the good sleeper is able to settle herself again, while the disturbed sleeper cries out for comfort.
- Possibly from a few weeks old, and certainly by the age of 2 months, all babies have the ability to soothe themselves back to sleep when they wake. This applies to day- or night-time sleeps – hence the need to find ways to teach your baby the difference between night and day, and encourage her to look forward to getting most of her sleep requirement at night.
- 70 per cent of babies are said to sleep from midnight to 5am by the age of 3 months. By 6 months this figure has risen to 85 per cent.
- Most experts agree that by 6 months almost all infants are physiologically capable of sleeping through the night.

Broken nights

In one study, researchers found that two-thirds of parents of 18-month-old babies were woken regularly over the previous 12 months. Almost one family in five was woken more than once a night, while one family in 14 was woken three or more times a night.

11

Your baby's sleep requirements

Understanding how your baby sleeps is a good basis from which to encourage him to sleep more soundly. Although we are all unique, the amount and type of sleep we need to help us feel refreshed follow common patterns.

In the early days it may seem as if all your baby does is sleep and feed. Then, over the following weeks and months his sleep begins to fall into more established patterns, until by the time he reaches 18 months the amount of time he spends asleep every day has fallen to around 13½ hours.

Surprisingly, we still don't fully understand why we need to sleep. However, we do know that everyone's sleep falls into two distinct states: REM (Rapid Eye Movement) sleep and non-REM sleep.

Above Newborn babies sleep on average 16–17 hours a day.

REM sleep

REM sleep is an active state and is when we dream. It has been suggested that REM sleep has certain psychological functions, possibly allowing us to process and store our experiences. REM sleep is easy to identify in your newborn: his breathing is irregular, his body twitches and his eyes dart about under his eyelids. Your baby may be easily disturbed in this state.

Your baby developed REM sleep from around 6–7 months' gestation. Premature babies spend 80 per cent of their sleep in this state, full-term babies 50 per cent. It is still not known why young

Typical sleep requirements in babies

Age	Total sleep	Sleep (hours) Night sleep	Day sleep*
1 week	16½	8½	8 (4)
4 weeks	15½	8¾	6¾ (3)
3 months	15	10	5 (3)
6 months	14¼	11	3¼ (2)
9 months	14	11¼	2¾ (2)
12 months	13¾	11½	2¼ (2)
18 months	13½	11½	2 (1)

* Figure in brackets denotes number of roughly equal blocks.

Note: These are typical figures only — your baby may sleep more or less than this.

babies spend so much of their sleeping time in REM sleep, but it has been argued that it is necessary for their development. By the time your child is 3 years old, roughly one-third of his sleep will be REM sleep. He will reach the adult proportion of one-quarter of his sleep being REM sleep by later childhood or adolescence.

Right Most babies move their longest sleep to night-time by the age of a few months.

13

Above *Your baby may rouse as she moves between the phases of her sleep cycle, but as she gets older she will learn to fall back to sleep again.*

Non-REM sleep

The non-REM stage might also be described as 'deep sleep': it is the state in which we are most restful, lying quietly with regular heart rate and breathing patterns. There is very little dreaming. It is thought that during this stage most of the restorative function of sleep occurs.

In babies and young children, non-REM sleep is referred to as 'quiet sleep'. In this state, your baby will breathe deeply and lie very still. Occasionally you may see her make fast sucking motions, and now and then a sudden body jerk.

Adult non-REM sleep is divided into four different phases, each representing a different level of sleep, from drowsiness to deep sleep. Babies do not develop these distinct phases fully until they are about 6 months old. It is very difficult to rouse a child in the deepest stage of non-REM sleep.

Your baby's sleep cycles

As your baby sleeps, she will move progressively through the different phases of sleep. Newborns enter REM sleep immediately after falling asleep and move from deep to light sleep in cycles of roughly 20 minutes. By the time your child is about 3 months old, she will enter non-REM sleep first, a pattern that will continue for the rest of her life. As she grows, her sleep cycles will also become progressively longer: when she reaches school age, they occur every hour or so; by the time she becomes an adult, these cycles will last for around 90 minutes or more.

It is very common for both adults and children to rouse as they move into the next phase of their sleep cycle. This explains why your newborn may only seem to sleep deeply for 20 minutes before waking again. As your child gets older, you may even find that she sits up in bed and adjusts her covers before lying down and progressing to the next level of sleep. This is perfectly normal.

It also gives us a clue as to how to encourage your baby to sleep well at night. If brief night-time 'wakings' are perfectly natural, even in adults who profess to be sound sleepers, what you have to do is persuade your baby to take them in her stride and allow herself to fall back to sleep and into the next stage of her sleep cycle.

'I used to get frustrated when Aidan was tiny. It would seem that almost as soon as he had gone off to sleep he was awake again, crying for me. I couldn't get anything done. So I started ignoring him for a few minutes, just to get the chore finished that I had started. And I found that quite often, the crying would stop because he'd sent himself back to sleep again.'

Marianne Fowler, mother of Aidan (1½)

Left As your baby grows, her sleep cycles will change.

15

Where will your baby sleep?

It's the dilemma that all new parents ponder over: where will your baby sleep? There is no right answer, and each family works out their own solution. You may have very clear ideas about where you want your baby to sleep, or you may want to adopt a trial-and-error approach to see what works best for you.

Basically, you have four options:
- In your bed.
- In his own bed in your bedroom.
- In a bedside cot.
- In his own room.

There are advantages and disadvantages to each solution, but none of them should affect your baby's ability to sleep or the strategies available to you to encourage him to sleep. However, whichever option you choose it is vital that you follow the essential safety guidelines to help keep your baby safe at night (see pages 20–21).

In your bed

Bed sharing has become more fashionable over recent years, and some experts argue that it is the most natural solution for parents and babies. It is certainly true that, until comparatively recently, many

Left Tell-tale signs that your baby is ready to sleep include floppiness, irritability and rubbing his eyes with his hands.

children would have shared their parents' bed during their early years because there simply wasn't the room for them to sleep elsewhere. It is also true that bed sharing is still the norm in many cultures today.

However the Foundation for the Study of Infant Death (FSID) disputes claims that having your child in your bed reduces the risk of cot death. The largest recent study into this subject found that if all the safety guidelines are followed (see pages 20–21), babies who share their parents' bed are at no less, and no greater, risk of cot death than those who sleep in a separate cot in their parents' room.

Pros
- Very cosy.
- Makes night feeds easy, especially if you are breastfeeding.

Cons
- Must follow the safety advice (see pages 20-21).
- Not appropriate if you and/or your partner smoke.

'We started off trying to get the boys to sleep in their own beds, but it just didn't work. Then I read a book about co-sleeping and it gave me the confidence to do what I felt intuitively was right, which was to have them in with us. We put two king-size beds together and all slept together. And it was great: the boys were happy, so they slept, which meant we got a decent night's sleep. The older two gradually migrated into their own rooms when the time was right for them, but Patrick is still in with us.'

Wendy, mother of Edward (7), Thomas (4) and Patrick (3)

In her own bed in your bedroom

Putting your baby to sleep in her own bed (cot, carrycot or Moses basket) in your room is the safest solution for her. Research has shown that this can reduce the chance of cot death – in fact, the FSID recommends this option for babies under 6 months old.

Pros
- May reduce the risk of cot death.
- Easy to respond to your baby's needs at night.

Cons
- May be disruptive if your baby is a very light sleeper.
- Still have to get your baby used to her own room eventually.

'After reading about cot death, we decided Hannah should sleep in her carrycot in our bedroom at first. We worried that we would disturb her, but she only woke up when she needed to – for a nappy change or a feed – not because of us. She was only a couple of months old when she first slept through the night, and made the move into her own room quite happily after 6 months.'

Catherine, mother of Hannah (3)

In a bedside cot

Some manufacturers now make special 'bedside cots' with removable sides, so that you can share the cosiness of having your baby next to you while having her on her own mattress. However, some paediatricians are concerned that babies may get trapped in the space between the two mattresses, so it is vital to make sure they are pushed right up against each other.

Pros
- Easy to check on your baby in the night.
- Cosy.

Cons
- Your baby could get trapped between the two beds.
- No known value in reducing the risk of cot death.

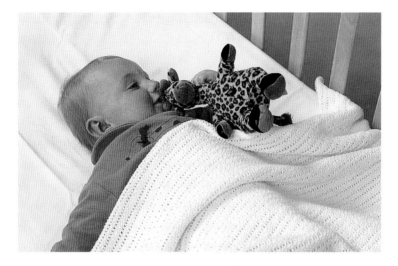

In her own room

For some parents this is the only solution – for example, if your own bedroom is too small to accommodate your baby as well. You may also think this is the only option if you or your partner works antisocial shifts. However, there is research which suggests that having adults coming and going at all hours could help to protect your baby, possibly because she is under more constant surveillance. If you do decide to put your baby in her own room, use a baby monitor to 'listen' in to her and make sure that you respond when she needs you.

Above Unless your baby shares your bed, you will have to invest in a cot at some point.

Pros
- No tiptoeing around your baby at night.
- No need to get her used to her own room later.

Cons
- Slightly higher risk of cot death than if she is in her own bed in your room.
- Means stumbling to the nursery for night-time changes and feeds.

Sleeping safely

Medically known as Sudden Infant Death Syndrome (SIDS), the words 'cot death' strike fear into every parent's heart. Although the number of babies claimed by SIDS is very small, the rates do vary around the world – from 1 in 4,000 infants in Finland and the Netherlands, 1 in 2,000 in the UK, to 1 in 700 in the United States and 1 in 400 in Italy. Babies under the age of 6 months are most at risk. However, the Foundation for the Study of Infant Death urges that there are steps you can take to minimize the risks for your baby.

Essential safety guidelines

- **Put your baby to sleep on his back on a flat mattress, without a pillow.** You may find he rolls over during the night. If this happens, turn him onto his back again, but don't feel you need to keep checking him all night. When he can roll from back to front and front to back, continue to put him to sleep on his back, but then allow him to find his own position.
- **Keep his head uncovered.** Position your baby feet-to-foot – that is, with his feet at the bottom of his bed. This helps to minimize the chances of him worming his way under the covers.
- **Always use sheets and blankets rather than a duvet.** Make sure they are firmly tucked under your baby's shoulders so that he can't wriggle underneath them.
- **Babies find it difficult to regulate their body heat, so keep your baby's room at the right temperature, 16–18°C (61–64°F).** At this temperature, he should be dressed in a nappy,

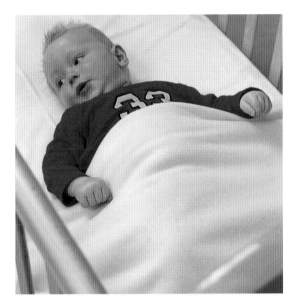

Left *Position your baby with his feet at the foot of his bed to minimize the possibility of him wriggling his way under the covers.*

vest and babygro, and have two to three light blankets for cover.

- **Monitor the temperature of his room with a nursery thermometer.** Position it near your baby's head, so that you are recording the temperature around his bed rather than on the other side of the room.
- **Do not put your baby's bed next to a radiator – he may overheat.** Similarly, do not put his bed up against a window – he may be in a draught during the winter, and may overheat if put down for a daytime nap in the summer.
- **When checking to see if your baby is too warm or too cold, always feel his tummy or the back of his neck rather than his hands or feet,** as these can appear icy even when he is too hot. Add or take off layers as appropriate.
- **Do not let anyone smoke near your baby.**
- **Do not allow yourself to fall asleep with your baby on the sofa or in an armchair.**

In your bed

If your baby is sleeping in your bed, it is important to ensure that his head is not near the pillow, and to use sheets or blankets rather than a duvet. Also, you must not share your bed with your baby if you or your partner is a smoker, has recently drunk alcohol, or is taking medication that may make you feel tired. It is also inadvisable for your baby to sleep in your bed if he was born before 37 weeks, weighed less than 2½ kg (5½ lb) at birth, or is less than 3 months old.

If it all gets too much

Most of us can pace ourselves through a few broken nights. The problems set in when the disruption continues. Tiredness becomes exhaustion, and you may find yourself showing symptoms similar to depression: anxiety, apathy or even violence.

Above If your baby is awake and screaming, then you'll be awake too. If you find that you can't cope, it is vital that you get help.

These feelings may be strongest in the early hours of the morning, when you are battling yet again with a wailing or wakeful child who is showing no signs of going to sleep. But no matter how frustrated or desperate you feel, it is vital never to shake your baby: research has shown that just one shake could cause her permanent brain damage.

Get help

If you are unable to suppress your feelings, it is vital that you get help by waking your partner, calling a friend, relative or neighbour, or telephoning the relevant helpline. You may not want to disturb other people in the middle of the night, but they would far rather lose a night's sleep than know that you returned to a situation with which you were truly unable to cope.

Prevention

Better still is to try to take steps to overcome your sleep deprivation before it reaches crisis point. For example:

- Catch up on lost sleep when your baby naps during the day.
- Let your partner take over during the evening while you go to bed, so that you have some reserves to see you through the night.
- Express some milk and share the night feeds

Tips for success

If you find yourself at breaking point, try the following routine:

1 Put your baby in her cot, leave the room and close the door – it won't hurt her to cry on her own for a few minutes, whereas one action from you could have irreversible consequences.

2 Make yourself a drink (non-alcoholic – it's important that you stay in control) and sit quietly while you calm down, preferably somewhere where you can't hear your baby.

3 Do not return to your baby until you feel able to cope with her.

with your partner, so that you each get a chunk of unbroken sleep.

- Ask for (or buy in) help: new grandparents or friends would probably love the chance to cuddle your baby for a few hours while you catch up on some sleep.

If you are on your own, not all these suggestions will be relevant. However, there are additional steps you can take to make sure you have the support you need to see you through (see pages 84–85).

Right *The most loving of parents can reach the end of her tether after weeks or months of broken sleep.*

preparing
for sleep

2

- Everyone is different

- Getting ready for sleep

- Creating the right atmosphere

- Ready for sleep:
  questions and answers

Everyone is different

Sleep is a universal need, and it's not just parents who end up grumpy when their sleep is broken. Research shows that babies who sleep well at night are more likely to be contented during the day, while those who sleep poorly are more likely to be irritable. This is why adopting strategies to help your baby sleep soundly benefits both of you.

Above *Although all babies have the same fundamental needs, each one is unique.*

But although we all need sleep, and it is helpful to talk about the average sleep needs of babies, there is no such thing as an 'average' baby. This becomes more obvious if you have two or more children. Your first-born may be content to be put down awake in his cot, sucking his thumb happily for half an hour before drifting off, while your second may scream herself to exhaustion before falling asleep.

Equally, there is no such thing as an 'average' parent. Your neighbour may insist that controlled crying is the secret to getting your child to sleep successfully, but if you simply can't bear to hear your baby crying it may not be the right approach for you. Similarly, you may be keen to get your child to settle early so that you can have your evenings to yourself, but your friend may be happy for her baby to go to bed later because she is at work all day.

In short, all babies and all parents are unique. This is why this book contains a number of different strategies and advice on how to apply them, enabling you to choose the one best suited to you and your family. They can all be applied to babies and children of any age, either to encourage good sleeping habits from birth or to break a pattern of never-ending bedtimes or broken nights.

Your choice

Before you begin putting any sleep training into practice, you need to be honest with yourself. Take the following preliminary steps towards your goal:

1 Work out your strengths and weaknesses as a parent (we all have them).

2 Write down what ideally you would like to achieve: is it more important to you to have unbroken sleep from midnight, or for your baby to go to bed at 7pm, even if that means he might wake for further feeds in the night?

3 Use this frank assessment to decide which method is likely to be most successful for you and then adapt it, if necessary, to suit your family's specific needs.

Whatever you do, don't go down one route because you feel you ought to, or because other people insist it's the right one. Then, once you have made up your mind which strategy you are going to adopt and what your ground rules are, be prepared to stick to them.

Below You may be happy for your child to go to bed later so that you can have a family meal together in the evenings.

Getting ready for sleep

If you are one of those who collapse exhausted onto the sofa at the end of the day, you may feel you are only too ready for sleep – but preparing to get your baby to sleep well is another matter.

Whichever strategy you adopt, there are some key areas to be addressed beforehand that will give you a better chance of success.

Below Ask a friend or relative to babysit for a couple of hours during the day so that you can catch up on sleep.

Commitment

Teaching your baby to sleep well won't happen instantly. If you have already been through a prolonged period of broken sleep, following a sleep plan that could make your nights deteriorate initially takes real resolve. Starting a new sleep plan only to abandon it a couple of days later will do neither you nor your baby any good. What's more, it is likely to be even harder next time you try, because your baby knows that within a couple of nights you'll give in. **Strategy** Make sure both you and your partner are committed to your strategy before you begin.

Organization

You may reach the end of your tether and decide that tonight's the night to take action, but if you've got an early start ahead you may find your resolve waning in the small hours. Similarly, you may also be aware that you are going to lose some of your evenings as your try to settle you baby.

Strategy Try to introduce your new sleep strategy at a time when you have few other commitments (or, at least, fewer than normal). Stock up your freezer with instant meals, or eat your main meal at midday.

Above You need to make sure that your child can come to no harm if she can climb in and out of bed.

Support

If your baby has an established pattern of poor sleeping at night, the initial days of sleep training can be hard for both you and her. This may leave you both groggy the next day. To help in this situation, you will need as much back-up as possible through this crucial time.

Strategy Ask friends, relatives or neighbours to babysit for a couple of hours during the day, so that you can catch up on some sleep.

Safety precautions

All successful sleep strategies involve leaving your baby alone eventually. You cannot do this if you worry that she might harm herself.

Strategy Make sure her bed is safe by following the essential safety guidelines on pages 20–21, and that there are no toys in it on which she might choke or hurt herself. If your child is in a bed she can climb out of, make sure that her room is safe. If she can readily reach the stairs, make sure these are blocked with a secure safety gate.

29

Creating the right atmosphere

We often think that young babies can sleep anywhere, but there are lots of factors that can make it difficult for your baby to sleep without interruption. So, try to make the environment in which he spends his nights as conducive to unbroken sleep as possible.

Outside lights

Early morning sunlight as well as street lights or flashing headlights could disturb your baby.
Strategy Consider installing a black-out blind at his window or tacking black-out lining fabric behind his existing curtains.

Below If your children always wake early, check whether something is disturbing them first thing in the morning.

Central heating

If your heating clicks into action at 5.30am every day, it's probably no coincidence that this is when your baby gives you his early morning wake-up call.
Strategy Try setting the heating to come on a little bit later. If you think your baby will get too cold as a result, leave a small electric heater on a low setting in his room overnight. But make sure that your baby's room is neither too hot nor too cold as a result of this, as babies are unable to regulate their own body temperatures effectively (see the essential safety guidelines on pages 20–21).

Loud noises

Barking dogs, car engines, other family members – there are many

Left *Your child will be reassured if he can see his favourite toys when he goes to bed or wakes up.*

sudden noises that might startle your baby awake during his sleep.

Strategy While you may not be able to control many of these, it could be that repositioning your baby's bed or putting him to sleep in a quieter room will enable him to sleep more soundly. You can also encourage him to become more used to regular household noises by allowing them to go on as normal when he is sleeping: vacuuming outside his bedroom door as he takes a daytime nap should ensure he is less readily disturbed by the noise!

A welcome haven

You also need to make his bedroom somewhere he wants to be.

Strategy Decorating his nursery in welcoming colours and positioning favourite toys within view of his bed will make it more inviting; if he sleeps in your room, try hanging a mobile over his bed to give him something on which to focus. Playing in your baby's room during the day will provide positive associations that he can carry with him through the night.

'Eleanor had always been a good sleeper until we moved house, just after her first birthday. Then she started waking at the crack of dawn every day. Once we worked out that the early morning trains were disturbing her, we moved her into the spare room, and she began to follow her old sleep patterns again.'

Amy, mother of Eleanor (2)

Ready for sleep:
questions and answers

Q Should I leave a light on for my baby at night?

A Putting your child to bed confidently in the dark gives her the message that it is a safe place to be and reduces the chances of her developing a fear of the dark. What's more, your child's body produces more of its own natural sedative, melatonin, in the dark, which in turn helps to settle her. However, you may feel that a small light makes it easier for you to check on your baby during the night.

Set the lights how you want them before your child falls asleep, otherwise she will wonder why it's all different when she wakes during the night. Make sure the light it is no stronger than 15W (the plug-shaped lights that connect directly into electric sockets are ideal): research suggests that babies and young children who sleep with the light on are more likely to be short-sighted than those who sleep in the dark.

Q Should I let my baby have a dummy at night?

A Research suggests settling your baby to sleep (day and night) with a dummy can slightly reduce the risk of cot death, even if the dummy falls out while your baby is asleep. However, the risk of cot death greatly reduces after six months, so it is recommended that you wean your baby off it after this point, especially as there can be complications with long-term dummy use. It can affect how your child's teeth grow, which could lead to dental complications later on. And the

Below *A dummy may comfort your child, but could present other problems.*

longer you allow your child to have a dummy, the more of a crutch it will become for her – and you may find yourself getting up several times a night to retrieve it for her from underneath the blankets. Try introducing an alternative comforter, for example a suitable, safe toy, or perhaps an old or well-worn item of clothing that has that familiar smell of mum or dad – but make sure there is no danger of your child ending up covered by her comforter.

Q My baby and toddler have to share a room – will they disturb one another?

A Children have shared rooms successfully for generations, and there is no reason why yours can't do the same. Many parents find their children are able to sleep quite happily through any night-time disturbances from their siblings. In fact, putting your baby in with her sibling may help to settle her, as she will naturally fall in with their established, rhythmic breathing.

However, if you intend to start sleep training one child, it may be an idea to move your other child to another room – you don't want to compromise your new sleep programme through fear that your other child might be disturbed. If you have to move a younger child temporarily, she should be able to take it in her stride, but an older child may be less willing to give up her bedroom. Appealing to her maturity may work: explain why you need her to swap beds for a few nights, and how she can be a big help to you in this. Or try to build in some extra treats for her, such as an extra story at bedtime while she is in her temporary bed. You should be able to put your children back in together again within a few nights.

Above *Your baby and toddler should be able to share a room without disturbing one another unduly.*

a good night's sleep

- Tackling your baby's sleeping habits
- Establishing a bedtime routine
- The link between feeding and sleep
- Learning to settle
- Method 1: controlled crying
- Method 2: repetitive reassurance

3

- Method 3: the carrot approach

- Method 4: gradual withdrawal

- Towards uninterrupted nights

- Dealing with disruptions

- Troubleshooting

Tackling your baby's sleeping habits

You've done your preparations: you've worked out what sleep pattern you want to aim towards, you've made your baby's room cosy and inviting, and you've got friends and relatives on standby to give you the help you need. Now you really are ready to tackle your baby's sleeping habits. Just remember: you could be only a few days away from a really good night's sleep!

Below Strictly functional night feeds will help your baby to understand that you want him to go back to sleep.

Night-time is for sleeping

The first thing you need to do if you want your baby to sleep well at night is to teach him that night-time is for sleeping. It may sound obvious, but you'd be surprised how many new parents overlook this.

It's easy to understand how this blurring of day and night arises. If you have no real experience of babies and your newborn insists at 2am that he wants to play, you may think this is what you, as a parent, should do. The problem is that after a few nights your baby will be looking forward to his early-hours play session, and will be waking up in anticipation of it.

Steps to success

Fortunately, it shouldn't take long to teach him that night-time is for sleeping.

1 Keep night feeds and nappy changes functional: use only low lighting, try not to talk to your baby (if you do have to talk, keep your voice flat and low) and don't make eye contact with him.

2 Do not begin any 'daytime' activity once you have fed and changed him; instead, put him straight back into his bed.

Left Playing with your child during the day will help to tire her out ready for bedtime.

3 If he tries to engage you in play, resettle him using your chosen method (see pages 42–51).

By contrast, stimulate and engage your baby as much as possible during the day. This will not only give him the message that days are for socializing, fun and learning, but will also encourage him to be awake more during the day, which in turn will mean he is more tired by the evening.

Defining daytime naps

It is helpful if you can draw a distinction between night sleep and daytime naps. Try:

- Putting your baby to sleep in his carrycot during the day, rather than in his cot or Moses basket.
- Drawing the curtains at night only.

'With Robert, we followed his lead and played when he wanted to. It took a long time for him to have clearly defined days and nights. With Toby, we were adamant we were not going back to such broken nights. Right from the start, we turned the lights off at night and kept night changes and feeds to the bare minimum. We didn't talk to him or look him in the eye. By the time he was only a few days old he knew he wasn't going to get anywhere with us at night, so he might as well sleep!'

Rebecca, mother of Robert (5) and Toby (3)

37

Establishing a bedtime routine

Babies and small children love routine: it helps them to make sense of their world and gives definition and shape to their day. This is as true of bedtime as of any other part of the day.

Above *Putting her toys away can help signal to your child that daytime is over.*

A clear routine will help your child to understand that in the daily sequence of events, the next stage is bed and sleep. Understanding this will in itself go some way towards setting her up for a good night's sleep. You can also take your routine with you when you go away, making it easier to settle your child in unfamiliar places.

Establishing a successful routine

Your bedtime routine should be predictable and enjoyable; it should also aim to calm your child down, rather than get her excited. Possible elements include:

- Tidying away toys.
- A relaxing bath.
- A drink (your baby should only have milk or water after her teeth have been brushed).
- A bedtime story.

It doesn't matter exactly what you do: what is important is that you do the same things in the same order every night, preferably at the same time. (You may also find that putting your baby down for her daytime naps at the same time every day helps her bedtime become more settled.)

Once your routine is well established, you can be a little more flexible – for example, you may feel that on some nights your child is too tired for a bath – but aim to be consistent for the first few months.

Very small babies

Some parents wait until their child is a few months old before establishing a bedtime routine, but there is no reason why you can't adopt one from the start. However, with a tiny baby, you need to give some thought to the timing of your routine.

You may decide to implement it in the early evening and treat all changes and feeds from then on as night activities (see pages 36–37). Alternatively, as 70 per cent of babies sleep from roughly midnight until 5am by the age of 3 months, you may want to run your bedtime routine just before the start of this 'core' sleep and then move it forward by half an hour every few days to extend her night sleep time gradually.

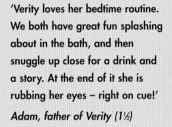

'Verity loves her bedtime routine. We both have great fun splashing about in the bath, and then snuggle up close for a drink and a story. At the end of it she is rubbing her eyes – right on cue!'
Adam, father of Verity (1½)

Left *A bath can encourage your baby to wind down before bedtime.*

The link between feeding and sleep

Successful feeding is essential for quiet nights: after all, your baby can't sleep through the night if he's hungry.

The early days

If you can, it is best for your baby if you can breastfeed him, but getting the hang of this can take a while. If you have any problems breastfeeding, your midwife or a voluntary breastfeeding counsellor will be happy to help. Even when you are both comfortable feeding, your baby is still likely to be hungry every couple of hours at first, as his tiny tummy simply can't hold enough milk to keep him going for longer.

As he grows, and is able to take bigger feeds, they should naturally become more spaced out. As he becomes more wakeful during the day he should also gradually adjust his feeding pattern so he's getting the majority of his feeds during the day, giving him less need to wake at night.

Left *Breastfeeding your baby strengthens your bond and is the best source of nourishment for your child.*

Weaning

Most experts agree that nearly all babies are physiologically ready to sleep through the night from six months. But current advice is not to wean before six months, and many babies continue to wake at night for feeds until they have solids.

By 1 year old your baby should have adopted your pattern of eating: three meals a day plus a couple of healthy snacks. During the transitional stage from 6 to 12 months, it's important to get the right balance between milk and solids. Your health visitor can advise you how to wean successfully and exactly what you should be giving him at each stage. But if he still seems very hungry at night, you may like to discuss ways to encourage him to take more solids during the day, and so reduce his need for night feeds. For example you might offer him solids first, so he's not tempted to fill himself up on milk.

'At 9 months Lily was still waking every two hours for a breastfeed, so my health visitor suggested we keep a feeding diary. It soon transpired that although Lily was enjoying three meals during the day she was hardly drinking anything at all as she was getting so much liquid at night. My husband agreed to go to her at night armed with only a bottle of water: after just two nights we never heard a peep out of her. She decided the water wasn't worth waking up for and started drinking during the day instead.'

Sally, mother of Lily (3)

Learning to settle

Teaching your child to send herself to sleep is the basis of all successful sleep-training strategies. You have a choice of methods – these are explained on the following pages – but if you want to enjoy unbroken nights you do not have a choice about the lesson!

We have already discovered that babies sleep in short cycles, and it is quite natural for them to wake briefly as they move from one cycle to the next (see pages 12–15). As she stirs, your baby will check that things are as they were when she went to sleep. If you always rock or feed her to sleep, she will be distressed when she realizes you are no longer there. Quite understandably, she is going to cry out for you. You will then have to comfort her back to sleep again. And so a vicious circle begins.

If, on the other hand, your baby learns to settle herself, when she rouses during the night she will discover each time that everything is as she last saw it. This will make it much easier for her to settle herself again and drift naturally into the next phase of her sleep cycle.

The cardinal rules

Before you decide which sleep-training method is for you, here are some basic rules to follow for teaching your child to settle herself:

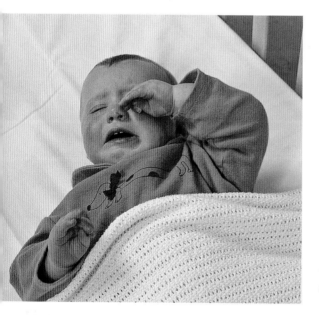

Left *If you hold your baby to sleep she is likely to miss your comforting presence when she stirs in the night.*

1 **Always put your baby to bed awake.**
If she tends to drift off during her feed, try ending the feed slightly earlier (she will have already had her fill), or tickle her toes as you put her down.

2 **Always put your baby to bed with the same special bedtime phrase.** Repeat this phrase whenever you have to put her back to bed, so that it acts as a reassuring sleep 'trigger' for her.

3 **Always settle your child in the same way,** whether you are putting her to bed for the night, putting her down for a nap in the day, or resettling her after a disruption at night (although you may want to reword your bedtime phrase slightly for a daytime sleep).

4 **If you go in to resettle her, try to do so without picking her up.**

5 **Do not alter her room once she has gone to sleep:** do not start switching lights on or off or rearranging furniture, as this will make it difficult for her to resettle when she stirs between sleep phases.

When can I start?

It is never too early to teach your baby to settle herself. After all, if she never has any association of being comforted to sleep, she is never going to miss it. However, if your child is under the weather, you should delay starting any new programme until she is fully recovered, otherwise it may be difficult to be sure if any distress is simply due to her adjusting to the new routine or because she is in discomfort.

Method 1: controlled crying

This widely advocated method for settling your child has fans worldwide. It should prove effective within a few nights.

Method: Leave your baby to cry for increasing periods of time, the principle again being that he will eventually give up and go to sleep.

Before you begin, decide how long you can bear to leave your baby crying initially: ideally, this should be five minutes, but must be at least one minute.

Below Use your special bedtime phrase each time you settle your child – but avoid picking him up.

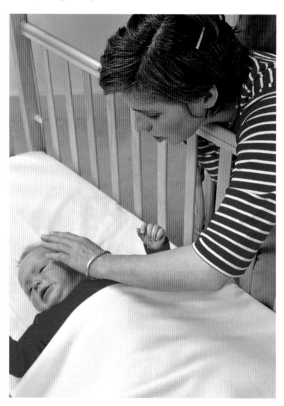

After settling him, leave the room and do not return until your predetermined time has elapsed. After resettling him, leave him for a slightly longer period: ideally, this should be five minutes longer than the first time, but must be at least one minute longer. Repeat this until you are leaving your baby for a maximum time of 20 minutes on the first night.

You can either repeat this on subsequent nights, or gradually increase the length of time for which you leave your baby before checking on him. So: on night two, do not go to him initially until 10 minutes has elapsed, extending to a maximum interval of 25 minutes; on night three, do not go to him initially until 15 minutes has elapsed, extending to a maximum interval of 30 minutes; and so on.

Tips for success

- Follow the cardinal rules for settling your baby every time you go back to him (see pages 42–43).
- Use a watch to time the intervals before you go to him – it can be very hard to listen to your baby crying, and you may otherwise find yourself going in much sooner than you intended.
- As the controlled crying can go on for a couple of hours initially, try to get on with something else in between going in to settle your baby, so that you don't become resentful of the time it is taking.
- Do not go back in to him (even if the allotted time has elapsed) if he appears to be settling – a visit from you could prompt him to start crying all over again.

Possible pitfalls

- You may worry that your baby will hurt himself through crying. However, there is no research to back this up: in fact, as long as there is no serious underlying cause, such as illness, crying is a sign that your baby is healthy and able to communicate.

Summary

- Popular method.
- Effective within a few nights.
- Can be time consuming initially.

Method 2: repetitive reassurance

This is an excellent alternative if you cannot bear to leave your baby crying at all. You should see a significant improvement within a week.

Method: Repeatedly reassure your baby that you are to hand, while at the same time insisting that it is time for her to go to sleep.

Settle your child in her bed, say your special bedtime phrase and head confidently towards the door. She will probably try to kick off the bedclothes or cry out for you. As soon as she does, return to her, resettle her, tuck her firmly back in, repeat your special bedtime phrase and go to leave once more. Repeat this for as long as it takes for her to go to sleep.

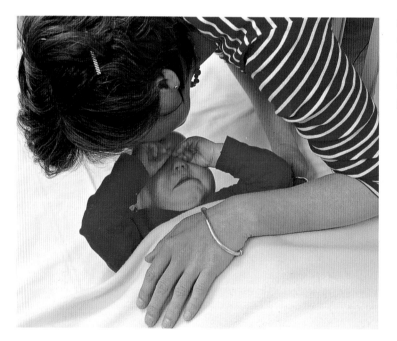

Left *Do not make eye contact or deviate from your chosen routine when reassuring your baby.*

Tips for success

- Follow the cardinal rules for settling your baby every time you have to resettle her (see pages 42–43).
- Do not 'reward' your child at any point when you go back to resettle her: do not make eye contact or allow your voice to become varied and engaging. The idea is that she should become bored with this before you do.
- This method can take a long time on the first couple of nights – you may not get as far as the door for the first hour! No matter how frustrating it is for you, you must remain calm and unruffled. If you begin to become stressed by the situation, your baby will pick up on it and will find it even more difficult to have the confidence she needs to go to sleep.
- This method also requires a lot of stamina if you have to resettle your baby during the night, so make sure you plan opportunities to catch up on sleep during the day.

Possible pitfalls

- This method can take a long time initially, which means less sleep than ever for you. Get as much back-up as possible and try to agree night shifts with your partner, so that you can both have some unbroken sleep during the night.
- Repetitive reassurance is not as quick as the cold turkey or controlled crying methods: you need to allow at least a week before judging the results.

Summary

- Does not require you to leave your baby to cry.
- Can be time consuming initially.
- Usually successful within a week.

Method 3: the carrot approach

This technique works through reward. It is particularly suitable if your child appears anxious, especially about bedtime.

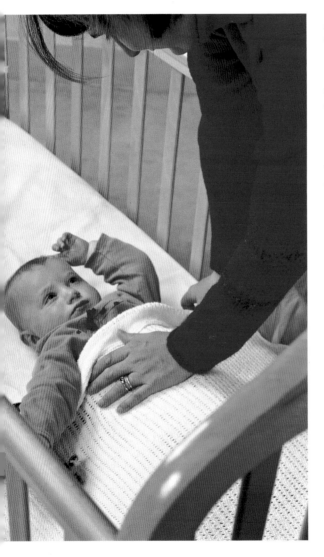

Method: After putting your child to bed with your special bedtime phrase, kiss him goodnight, promising to return in a minute to give him another kiss. Return almost immediately for the second kiss, then retreat a few steps, before returning for the next kiss. Put something away in his room, then return for the next kiss. Continue to kiss your baby at intervals as long as he remains in bed, with his head on the mattress. If he tries to get up, don't reprimand him – just steer him back under the covers and remind him that he only gets kisses if he stays in bed.

You should find that the number of kisses and the time it takes for your child to fall asleep reduce each night. Most children are sleeping easily within a week of adopting this approach.

Left *Patting your baby may be a more comfortable reward if you suffer from back ache.*

Tips for success

- Don't reward your child with anything other than quiet kisses. Cuddles, stories, chat and drinks are all out.
- Although this method is also known as the 'kissing game', do not allow it to degenerate into general bedtime frivolity. Be firm with the rules: your child only gets his reward if he lies quietly in bed.
- This method can take a long time on the first couple of nights, so be prepared. Steel yourself for up to 300 kisses over a three-hour period the first time you put your baby to bed in this way.
- Hold back from kissing your baby again if you think he is drifting off to sleep – you may rouse him unnecessarily.

Possible pitfalls

- If you suffer from backache, you may find all the bending down involved in this technique a strain. Try gently patting your baby's hand or head instead.
- Many children try to test their parents' resolve on around night five of this method, but if you can make it through this temporary upset you should be on the home straight.

Summary

- Reassuring for your baby.
- Initially demanding.
- Usually successful within a week.

Method 4: gradual withdrawal

This is a useful technique if you have become enmeshed in lengthy bedtime rituals, such as lying down with your baby to help her go to sleep. It works on the principle that a series of small changes is easier to get used to than one big one, but it may take weeks to be successful.

Method: Put your child to bed and then sit quietly by her as she falls asleep. Gradually, over the coming days and weeks, move further away from her bed, until eventually you are no longer in her room as she falls asleep.

Just how quickly you are able to move to the other side of the room and then out of the door will depend on how ingrained your current bedtime rituals are and how confident you feel. Your baby may resist each time you move your bedside vigil a little bit further away – if you remain calm but firm, this resistance should only last a night or two.

Tips for success

- Do not make eye contact or engage with your baby in any way while you remain in her room. Look away from her, or take a book in with you to read, so that she finds it more difficult to get your attention.
- Only move further away from your baby when she has got used to the previous position.
- Go at a pace your baby can manage. If she becomes really distressed every time you reposition yourself further away from her bed, move only a small amount every few nights. On the other hand, if she seems to be taking

Left *Reading a book can help you avoid eye contact with your baby.*

the changes in her stride, be confident about speeding up your retreat.

Possible pitfalls

- It is easy to become 'stuck' at any given point using this technique, so try not to lose track of the end game: move to your next position as soon as you feel your baby is ready.
- Your baby may show renewed distress when you make the final move to outside her bedroom door, so be prepared to 'keep guard' by her door for a few nights. After this, try getting on with some chores near her room, such as cleaning the bathroom or doing the ironing on the landing, so that she can be reassured you are still nearby. Eventually, you will be able to dispense with even this reassurance.

Summary

- A gentle technique.
- Can take a long time.

Towards uninterrupted nights

Congratulations! You are now well over half-way towards your target of uninterrupted nights.

If you have taught your baby that nights are for sleeping, he should be spending most of the night asleep. And if you have also taught him to settle himself when he stirs in the night, he is far more likely to drift happily back to sleep than to cry out

'Core' sleep

With the right sleep training, most babies develop a clear 'night sleep' of five or six hours uninterrupted sleep from just a few weeks old. Some sleep experts advise never feeding your baby again during these 'core' sleep hours, once they have been established.

Right Your baby is likely to continue to need night feeds until he is about 6 months old.

Left *You should find that the time between your baby's night feeds gradually increases as he grows.*

for reassurance. So, you should automatically find that the time between your baby's night wakings gradually increases, as he is able to slip naturally into the next stage of his sleep cycle.

Physiological constraints

Of course, for young babies the aim of sleeping through the night may still be some way off: if his tummy simply isn't big enough to sustain him through the night, he will still have to wake for feeds. As he grows, you should find the time between feeds gets progressively longer; you may even find he suddenly drops one of his night feeds of his own accord.

The good news is that by the age of 6 months most babies are physiologically capable of sleeping all night long. What's more, there are steps you can take to make sure your baby is one of those who achieves this goal as soon as his tummy enables him to go all night without a feed.

'William has only just started sleeping through, and the trick seems to have been stopping breastfeeding him at night. He was still waking up two or three times a night for feeds until a few weeks ago. I was beginning to think it was more for comfort than because he was hungry, but I wasn't sure. Then we moved house and the boys went to stay with my parents for four days. Obviously, they had to give him bottles at night and I decided to continue this when he came home. The first night he was home, William woke once for a feed. But when he got a bottle instead of my breast he didn't bother waking any more that night. What's more, we've not had a peep out of him at night since then.'

Natalie, mother of Miles (3) and William (8 months)

Night feeds

The first thing is to make sure you are only feeding your baby at night when she really is hungry. It is very easy to offer her a feed the moment she wakes – after all, you know it will settle her – but if you do she could end up waking from habit, rather than because she is hungry. And that's not doing either of you any favours.

Before you rush to give her milk, check whether there may be other reasons why she is awake. Is she wet or dirty? Is she too hot or too cold? Is she teething or suffering from wind? If you only feed your child when you are sure she needs it, you should again find the time between her night feeds increases, until from around 6 months old she abandons them altogether.

Tips for success

Some parents find their children cling to night feeds long after they really need them. If you suspect this is the case with your child, try:

- Offering her water instead of milk. If you don't feel happy making this switch overnight, gradually water down her milk.
- Being strict about feeding her in a chair and putting her straight back down in her own bed, rather than falling asleep with her in your bed.

If you are breastfeeding, try:

- Offering a bottle at night – it may reduce her incentive to wake up.
- Gradually cutting down the length of each feed.

Hold back

Many parents fall into the trap of rushing to their baby the moment she wakes at night. But we have already discovered that it is quite natural for babies to cry out at night, as they shift about in their

'When the twins were younger, my husband used to be 'on duty' for night feeds on Fridays and Saturdays. I noticed that they used to wake for a feed at around 2am on those nights, but not the rest of the week. I then realized they were waking on my nights, but as I was so tired I wasn't responding to them immediately and they were settling again. My husband agreed not to be so zealous about rushing straight through to them, and that was it – no more disturbed nights!'

Juliet, mother of Grace (3) and twins Jack and Rose (1)

sleep and move from one part of their sleep cycle to the next.

Try restraining yourself: wait five minutes before you go to her. You may well find that she goes back to sleep. And the more she gets used to resettling herself in this way, the more successful she will become at it.

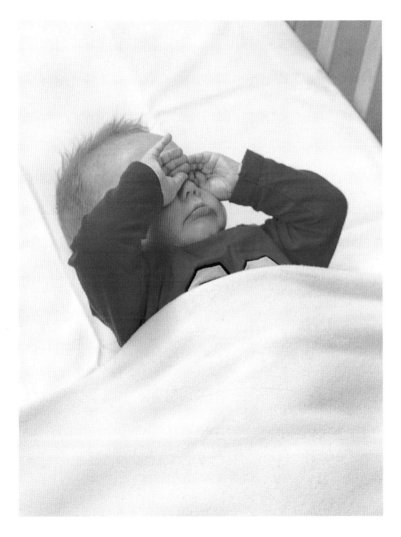

Left If you avoid rushing in to your baby, you may find that she resettles herself.

55

Dealing with disruptions

Unfortunately, the journey to uninterrupted nights is blighted by disruptions. However, as long as you have already introduced good sleeping practices there is no reason why you can't get back on track once the hurdles have been passed.

Routine disturbances

Night nappy changes and feeds are unavoidable in the early months, but they don't have to prompt a two-hour play session. If you keep them strictly functional, with the lights down low and avoiding eye contact with your baby, he will get the message that these are different from day changes and feeds.

Right *Keep fun and games for daytime nappy changes. Night-time changes should be strictly functional.*

Colic

Colic is a bit of a mystery: no one knows what causes it, and some experts refute its existence. That's not very helpful when your 2-month-old baby suddenly turns into a screaming machine every evening! Colic typically occurs in the early evening and makes babies cry hard, pulling their knees up into their abdomen. It can also make them reluctant to settle or feed. Most babies grow out of it within a couple of months.

Strategies:

- One theory is that colic is caused by a build-up of wind during the day. Giving your baby an anti-wind treatment, such as gripe water, may help. Positioning him so that he has gentle pressure on his stomach (for example, resting him over your shoulder or face down on your lap) and patting his back may also help relieve some of the pain.
- Most babies who suffer from colic develop it by a few weeks old, so if your child does suffer from it, it is likely to be before he has established true night-times – that is, before he starts getting the majority of his total daily sleep at night. While he is suffering from it, you really just have to go with the flow and accept disrupted evenings for a few weeks. When he does finally settle at the end of the evening, you can continue with your chosen sleep programme to encourage him to sleep well for the rest of the night. When he outgrows the colic, you can also start moving to earlier bedtimes.

Above If your baby suffers from colic, you may have to accept disrupted evenings for a few weeks.

'My health visitor advised me to change Eleanor's nappy after feeding her, so she was as dry as possible when I put her back down. But I found that if I changed her first, she was far more likely to go back to sleep easily.'

Marguerite, mother of Eleanor (2)

57

Teething

Teething can be a painful and protracted process.

Strategies:

- Infant paracetamol can take away the pain (but it is not suitable for babies under 3 months old). Teething gels can help numb your baby's gums – the effect only lasts for around 20 minutes, but it may be enough to get her back to sleep.
- Homeopathic remedies are also effective: if your baby is cutting her front teeth, try camomilla (widely available from chemists, health food stores and homeopathic pharmacists). For a slightly older baby cutting her molars, ask a homeopathic pharmacist for podophyllum. With both remedies, make sure you follow the recommended dosage.
- Stick as closely as possible to your sleep plan, while accepting that there will be times when she needs you to be with her.

Between teething bouts, return as quickly as possible to your established sleep strategy.

Short-term illness

Illness in babies and young children can take many forms, and the symptoms are often worse at night.

Strategies:

- If your baby is unwilling to sleep at night because she has been dozing during the day, sit quietly by her bed and urge her to be calm, even if she can't sleep.
- If she normally sleeps in her own room but you feel she is too ill to be left alone, setting up a camp bed for yourself in her room will cause less disruption than moving her into your bed.
- Stick as closely as possible to your established routine, and return to it properly as soon as you feel your child is well enough to do so.

Above *If your baby is under the weather she may well have more disturbed nights than usual.*

Although illness in children is always distressing and tiring for parents, it is usually short-lived. If you have already established positive sleeping practices, you should find your child returns readily to these once she is feeling better.

Long-term illness: asthma

If your child has asthma, coughing or sneezing at night may make it difficult for her to enjoy sleep.

Strategies:
- Keep soft furnishings to a minimum.
- Keep pets out of her bedroom.
- Use special anti-allergen bed linen.
- Vacuum her mattress regularly.

If your child has any other long-term condition that disturbs her sleep, discuss with your doctor or health visitor what you can do to reduce her symptoms at night to help her sleep better.

Away days

When away from home, try to stick as closely as possible to your child's established night-time routine.

Strategies:
- Get everything (such as her travel cot) ready before you begin putting her to bed, and make sure you take her comforter with you.
- You may want to be more flexible about her bedtime at such times. The more firmly established her nights already are, the less disruptive occasional deviations are likely to be. If you are still in the early weeks of a new sleep programme, you may have to accept that the penalty for breaking the routine could be the hard work you have to put in to get her back on course once home.

Take a break

Colic, teething and illness can be hard work for parents as well as babies. If you find the pressure is getting too much, take steps to give yourself a break (see pages 22–23).

Troubleshooting

No matter how frustrating the problems are that you encounter while teaching your child to sleep successfully on his own, just remember: there isn't one that hasn't been encountered – and solved – by other parents before you.

Two of the most common problems are clingy babies, whose sleep is disrupted because they are worried about being separated from their parent, and babies who are still feeding at night.

Clingy babies

Some babies are more clingy than others. Many become clingy at certain developmental stages: a key time is around 8 months, when your baby works out that you and he are not one and the same, but different people. Most babies deal with this realization by sticking even closer than usual to their parents; this phase tends to last for a couple of months and is known as 'separation anxiety'.

- **It is a good idea to teach your baby to send himself to sleep *before* he gets to this stage:** telling him that he has to settle himself is likely to be more difficult if he is showing anxiety whenever you leave him. However, it is not impossible to teach babies who are generally clingy to send themselves to sleep.

- **Choose a strategy that gives your baby the level of reassurance you think he needs** and allow more time before you judge the results. Your baby will come to understand that although you leave him, you are not abandoning him.

If you have already established a successful sleep programme, don't be surprised if it encounters a minor setback as your baby develops separation anxiety: half of all babies who are already sleeping well suffer disturbed nights between the ages of 7 and 9 months. Unfortunately, this may not be a one-off: there may be many different points throughout his first couple of years when your baby seeks extra comfort from you as he works out his place in the world – and he may ask for some of this at night.

Below *There may be times when your baby needs extra reassurance.*

- **Revive your original sleep strategy**, give your child the reassurance he needs and guide him back towards sleep. If he normally sleeps well, he will want to return to unbroken nights as much as you do, once he feels confident enough to do so.

Hungry babies

First of all, it is reasonable for your baby to require feeds at night until she is around 6 months old. However, if you think her night feeds are becoming protracted, try keeping a 24-hour feed/sleep diary. Note how she feeds (guzzling furiously or sucking intermittently) and for how long.

- **If she is merely suckling**, your baby is probably feeding for comfort, rather than hunger. Try ending her feeds when you feel she has had her fill, then use your chosen strategy to insist she goes back to sleep. Within a few nights she should come to terms with the shorter, more efficient feeds and should then start reducing

Right *Not all babies who wake for feeds beyond 6 months are truly hungry babies.*

Below *Most babies are physiologically capable of going without night feeds from around the time they start crawling.*

'Until he reached 9 months, Robert used to wake up every two hours throughout the night and the only thing that would settle him was a bottle of milk. From about 10 months he started going for around four hours before he woke up, but we were getting tired and really wanted him to go for longer, so we started reducing the amount of milk we gave him. We also watered it down, so it was less worthwhile him waking up. And eventually it worked – we got our first full night's sleep when he was 16 months old.'

Rowena, mother of Robert (2)

them, as she no longer has the incentive of comfort suckling.

- **If she is hardly drinking during the day but feeding through the night,** it may be that, rather than being a 'hungry' baby, she simply has a topsy-turvy feeding routine. To turn things round, try offering her water only at night or gradually water down her night feeds: she will soon compensate by feeding more during the day.

- **If your diary shows you that you really do have a hungry baby,** introducing foods that release energy slowly as you wean her, for example pulses and pasta, may help. You can also try gradually reducing the length of each night feed to see if you can encourage her to take in more during the day.

When nothing else seems to work

If you've followed the advice so far and your baby is still refusing to settle, you may need to consider alternative strategies.

- **If he had a difficult birth, he may be in discomfort.** A cranial osteopath may be able to relieve the pressure in his skull by very gentle manipulation to realign his bones.

- **Massage is also an effective way of relaxing anxious babies.** Ask your health visitor for details of your nearest baby massage class. You may like to combine massage with aromatherapy. Choose a relaxing essential oil that is suitable for use with babies and small children (such as lavender or camomile), dilute in the correct proportions in an appropriate 'carrier' oil (such as almond oil), and massage the mixture into your baby's skin. However, you must never use essential or aromatherapy oils on your baby if he is under 3 months

Left *Your child's diet can effect his sleep. If you suspect that your child has a food sensitivity then keep a diary of his diet and sleep to try and establish a pattern.*

Below *There may be many reasons why your baby won't settle. If you are unable to pinpoint the problem then consult your doctor or health visitor.*

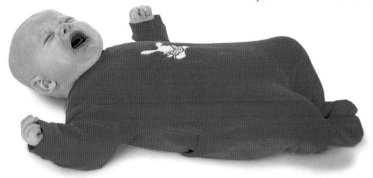

old without expert advice, and even after this age you must make sure you use them with proper care and caution. If you are in any doubt whether aromatherapy or a particular oil is appropriate for your child, consult a registered aromatherapist.

- **Your child may have a food sensitivity or allergy** that is making it difficult for him to sleep. Keep a diary of his diet and sleep to establish any correlation yourself, or ask your doctor to refer him to a dietician.

- **If your child appears restless and impulsive, he may be suffering from Attention Deficit Disorder (ADD).** If he seems very overactive, he may have the related Attention Deficit Hyperactivity Disorder (ADHD). If your child is diagnosed with ADD or ADHD, ask for specialist help to devise a sleep programme that will accommodate his needs.

If you haven't been able to pinpoint the problem, consult your doctor, or a specialist organization.

unbroken nights for older children

4

- Toddlers' sleep requirements

- It's never too late

- Rewards

- Troubleshooting

Toddlers' sleep requirements

The earlier you introduce good sleep habits, the better for you and your baby. But if you have a toddler who still wakes up several times a night, or a pre-school child who simply won't go to bed, don't despair! It is never too late to reclaim your nights for sleeping.

Not surprisingly, as your child grows his sleep needs change. Most significantly, you can expect him to cut out his daytime nap as his overall sleep requirements fall.

Dropping daytime naps
Your child will let you know when he is ready to reduce his daytime sleeps.

From two to one: When he is ready to cut back from two naps to one, you can expect him no longer to show signs of tiredness in the morning, but to fall asleep in the afternoon.
- You may need to move your lunchtime forward a little, otherwise there is a danger of him falling asleep at the table!

From one to none: Dropping his last nap can be a bit more of a problem. Your child may push his nap back later and later, until it begins to interfere with his bedtime. At this stage you may need to take the initiative to eliminate it.

Left Even boisterous toddlers can be introduced successfully to good sleep practices.

- Create gentle playing time to stimulate him, but don't embark on anything too boisterous – he is liable to be grumpy by late afternoon as his body adapts to life without a siesta, and rough and tumble games may well end in tears.
- You may find it difficult to keep your child awake if you take him out in the car or pushchair at his normal nap time – for example, if you have to pick up older children from school. If possible, try to alter your routine slightly for a couple of weeks while he gets used to his new sleep-free days. Perhaps you could ask someone else to pick up his older sibling. If this isn't possible, try to keep him awake by telling him stories or singing songs and playing observation games together.
- Finally, be prepared to start your child's bedtime routine earlier as he drops his daytime nap. Don't worry that this will mean he is up at the crack of dawn: although his total sleep requirement has fallen, he will still need to add some of his former day-sleep time to his night sleep in order to compensate for his lost nap, so he should in fact sleep for longer at night.

Above Your child should naturally reduce his day sleeps as he gets older.

Typical sleep requirements in toddlers and pre-school children

Age	Total sleep	Sleep (hours) Night sleep	Day sleep
18 months	13½	11½	2
2 years	13	11½	1½
3 years	12	11	1
4 years	11½	11½	-
5 years	11	11	-

Note: These are typical figures only – your child may sleep more or less than this.

It's never too late

If you've had a year or more of broken nights, you may feel that the goal of uninterrupted sleep is an unattainable dream. But even the most persistent poor sleeper can be taught to go to bed and stay there in a comparatively short space of time.

The fundamentals of getting a toddler or pre-school child to sleep through the night – even one who has never achieved this before – are essentially the same as training a baby to sleep well:

- **Your child needs to understand that nights are for sleeping:** if you let her run around after you've put her to bed, she is never going to understand that you really want her to stay there until morning.
- **You need to establish a positive, structured bedtime routine** to calm her down and act as a physical and mental trigger that bedtime is the next, immovable, part of her day.
- **You then need to teach her to settle on her own** (see pages 42–51). If she relies on your presence in order to get to sleep, she is going to suffer the same anxiety as a younger baby when she stirs in the night and realizes you are no longer there.

Left Most toddlers and older children enjoy having a bedtime story read to them as part of their bedtime routine.

'David used to be an appalling sleeper. It was our fault, really, as we thought broken nights were part of parenthood and put up with it. But by the time he was 3, we decided we had to take a stand. It was really hard work for a month, but after about four weeks he began to go to sleep without a fuss. He still doesn't sleep through every night, but it's dramatically better than it used to be.'

Melanie, mother of David (4)

Commitment

If your child has a long history of difficulty getting to sleep or broken nights, she is likely to resist a new sleep strategy more stubbornly than a young baby, so it will probably take you longer to get results. It is therefore even more vital that you have the back-up and resolve in place to enable you to see your chosen method through successfully (see pages 28–29). It may take you a couple of weeks to see significant results, but the important thing to hang on to is that you *will* get results, as long as you remain steadfast.

Above *You need to be firm if your child is reluctant to go to bed.*

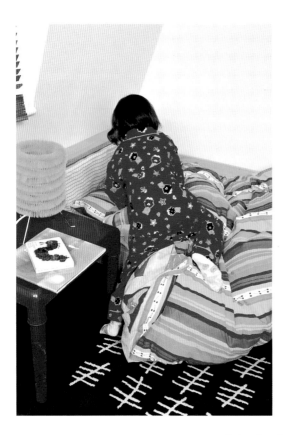

Above Getting out of bed is a favourite strategy among toddlers for delaying sleep.

Adapting sleep strategies

All the behaviour management strategies designed to teach babies to settle on their own (described on pages 42–51) can be used successfully with older children. Again, the principles are the same: analyse your family and your needs and choose the method you believe will work best for you, then follow it through. However, you may need to adapt the techniques slightly for older children.

Talk it through. Now that your child is able to communicate with you verbally, it is important for you to discuss things with him. **Strategy** Explain what is happening and why. Also make it clear that you are not going to be swayed in your resolve over this issue.

Jack-in-the-box. As well as resisting the new regime through crying, an older child might keep getting out of bed.
Strategy If this happens, resist any urge to pick him up, look sympathetic or even reason with him about why he needs to be in bed – it is important not to 'reward' him in any way. Instead, look firm and say simply 'Bed'. Turn him around, rest your hand lightly on his shoulder and steer him firmly back towards his bed. It is important to maintain this unruffled neutrality even if your child throws a tantrum while he is out of bed. When he sees that he gets no response from you, he will soon get bored and begin staying under his covers.

Prolonged bedtimes. An older child might also play games to drag bedtime out for longer. These might include claiming that he's hungry or thirsty, or that he needs another trip to the toilet.

Strategy To counter this, build any essential needs into his bedtime routine. Bedtime normally follows soon after tea for young children, so you know he's not hungry. Give him a last drink of water or milk before he begins his bedtime routine (if he is prone to becoming thirsty during the night, leave a beaker of water by his bed). Make sure he goes to the toilet before he gets into bed.

If you are confident his claims are merely an attempt to manipulate you, you can refuse to indulge them just as confidently. But don't get sidetracked into long negotiations or reasoning with him: tell him simply that he has just had a meal/ a drink/been to the toilet and repeat your bedtime phrase to him. He will soon get the message that you are not to be worn down.

Left Talking through your new night-time ground rules is important with older children.

73

Rewards

Rewards can be a powerful tool with which to help motivate your child. The older she is, the more sophisticated and long-term the rewards can be.

Above *A promised treat can really motivate an older child who can see the point of working towards a long-term goal.*

There are a variety of techniques you can use, but there are also some common rules for making them effective.

Ground rules

1 **Accentuate the positive.** Highlight your child's successes, not her failures. If she doesn't achieve her target, find something encouraging to say, rather than emphasizing that she has failed to earn her reward. For example: 'No, you didn't sleep all through the night, but you were up one less time than the night before, and I'm sure you'll manage it tonight.'

2 **Be consistent.** Don't keep changing what your child has to do to achieve her reward, or start adding extra conditions, such as 'I know you slept all night long, but now I want you to eat your breakfast as well or you won't get your star.'

3 **Don't punish.** Do not threaten to take her reward away once she has earned it or you will undermine her achievement.

4 **Be organized.** If you have promised your child a treat if she achieves her target, make sure you have it to hand in the morning. IOUs are not particularly appealing to young children.

5 **Think small.** A string of small rewards is generally more effective than one large one.

Different approaches

Decide which of the following techniques is likely to appeal most to your child, and then put it into practice:

- **Praise.** Don't you like being told when you've done something well? So will your child!
- **Cuddles.** Never underestimate the power of a cuddle – all it costs is your time.
- **Star chart.** Effective from around the age of 2 years: every time your child goes straight to bed or sleeps through, she gets a star. Pin up her chart in the kitchen where she can see it, and so that she can show off her achievements to visitors. After a certain number of stars, you could reward her with a small present.
- **Reward box.** Useful for children who think they are too old for star charts. Leave a small shoebox under your child's bed: if she achieves her target, slip in a small reward for her to discover in the morning. If she doesn't stay quiet during the night, it will remain disappointingly empty.
- **Special treat.** Great for children aged 5 years and up, who can see the point of working towards a long-term goal. Agree on a treat that appeals to her, such as inviting her friends over for tea, if she sleeps well for a week.

Below A cuddle from you is one of the best rewards your child can have.

Troubleshooting

Sleep training older children can produce more problems, simply because they have more ingenuity than babies. And even children who have previously been good sleepers can start throwing tantrums at bedtime as they try to carve out their own identity. But remember: you will always succeed in the end.

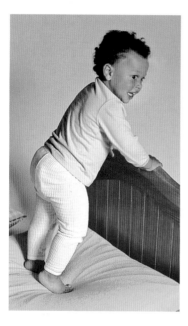

Above Some children will play up at bedtime for one parent but not for the other.

Tantrums at bedtime

Tantrums are common around the age of 2, when children really start to push the boundaries given to them.

Strategy The trick with all tantrums, including those at bedtime, is not to respond. If you get angry or try to cajole, your child has succeeded in getting a reaction from you, and will consider it worthwhile taking the same approach again.

He may well need to get his frustration out of his system, so let him work his way through his anger. Once he has calmed down, don't refer to the tantrum, but quietly pick up your bedtime routine where he interrupted it. He will naturally outgrow his tantrums – the less response he gets from you, the quicker this will happen.

Children who will only settle for one person

It can be heart-rending to hear your child screaming for you as your partner struggles to put him to bed. You could give in: after all, it's nice to feel wanted. Alternatively, you can ride it out. This has two advantages. Firstly, it enables you to start getting on with your own activities. Secondly, it eliminates a prop (that is, you) that your child needs in order to be able to get to sleep. The fewer props he relies on, the less likely he is to need those props during the night.

Strategy If you want to break the dependency, take it in turns with your partner to put your child to bed. On the nights when it is not your turn, be very strict that once you have said goodnight you don't reappear. Your child may scream the house down on the first few nights, but he will come to realize that you have not abandoned him and will learn to settle for your partner as well as you.

Going dry at night

This can throw even an established good sleeper out of his usual sleep pattern, especially if he has lots of accidents.

Strategy The best advice is to wait until he is really ready: dry nappies in the morning and waking to go to the toilet at night are the important signs. Invest in a mattress protector and deal with any accidents with minimum fuss. Encourage him to go straight back to sleep again using your normal phrase. You could also try a reward system (see pages 74–75).

Below 'Rewarding' your child if he has a tantrum may encourage him to have more.

Smooth transitions

Moving from her cot into a bed can be a major challenge, a complete non-event or a new adventure that can make your child feel very grown up.

Strategy If you have to move her because you are expecting another baby, do it well before your due date so that she doesn't think her new sibling has usurped her position. Explain to her what is happening and allow her to feel that she has some say in the matter: perhaps she can help to choose her bed or a new duvet cover. If she does have difficulties settling in her new bed, try playing games on it with her during the day so that it becomes a place she enjoys being.

Night fears

Older children can develop a range of night-time fears as their imaginations grow. Sometimes these occur in isolation, sometimes your child may exhibit a number of them at once.

Night fears may simply reflect your child's growing under-standing of the world. Sometimes they are triggered by images she has seen, so monitor your child's television viewing, particularly before bedtime.

Alternatively, night fears may be triggered by real anxieties in her life, such as starting nursery, the arrival of a new baby or stress within the family. If your child is going through a period of change that may be unsettling for her, reassurance during the day will be a big help in making her more confident at night. Without spoiling her, try to build some fun

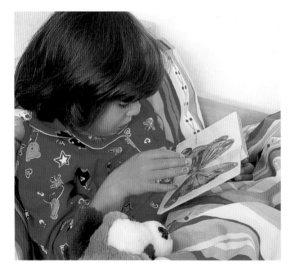

Above *The images your child sees before she goes to sleep can trigger related dreams.*

events into her day such as a trip to the park or a visit to friends, give her extra cuddles and tell her that you love her.

Fear of the dark It is important not to reinforce this, but to treat the dark as a warm and welcoming place in which you feel comfortable.
Strategy You can give your child a nightlight, but this confirms that the dark is something we need to banish. However, most children who rely upon nightlights grow out of them during their early years at school, when they realize the dark isn't something of which they need to be afraid.

Fear of monsters We give children conflicting messages about monsters. We read them stories about them, and then think they are silly when they worry that there are six-headed creatures lurking under their beds! You may know there aren't, but if you dismiss your child's fears you are giving her the message that you don't believe her.
Strategy Listen to her fears, but seek to dispel them. Look for monsters in the places she says they are hiding, to reassure her that there are none. If necessary, 'cast' a magic spell to keep monsters out of her room during the night, or position a trusted toy by her door to keep guard.

Right Moving out of his cot and into a new bed can cause your child anxiety.

Nightmares These are common from the age of 2 right through until the teenage years: half of all 5-year-olds have nightmares. They are generated during REM sleep, and are most likely to occur during the last two-thirds of the night. They are more likely to happen if your child is stressed or anxious; however, most nightmares have no cause and no real significance.

Strategy If your child wakes from a nightmare, go in and reassure him, tuck him back in, say your special bedtime phrase and leave the room as soon as you can. If your child has recurrent nightmares, keep a diary to see if there is a pattern. Repeated nightmares can often be controlled, as they occur in the lighter stages of sleep: for example, if your child dreams he is being chased by a bird, suggest that you both catch it in a cage.

Night terrors These are different from nightmares, although they can easily be confused with them. They can be traumatic to witness, especially as your child is unlikely to recognize you or want you to comfort him – he may, in fact, become more agitated if you try. However, your child will not remember a thing in the morning! This is because night terrors occur in the deepest part of sleep, usually in the first few hours after going to bed: although your child may appear to be awake, he isn't. He may seem very agitated and frightened, possibly screaming or moaning. However, as there is no dream occurring, when your child does wake he will not be scared (which you would expect if he had a nightmare); on the contrary, waking can provide immediate release from the night terror and he is likely to go back to sleep quickly.

Above *Your child is most likely to wake from a nightmare in the early hours of the morning.*

Strategy Although night terrors are disturbing to watch, your best response is to do nothing. If you do try to rouse your child before the episode has run its course, you may frighten him by your own anxiety. In addition, as your child won't remember the event, it will not cause him anxiety about going to bed on subsequent nights.

Sleepwalking

Sleepwalking is very common (one in six children sleepwalk at some stage, usually as they approach adolescence) and tends to run in families. Like night terrors, sleepwalking occurs in the first one-third of the night, when your

child is in deep sleep. However, it can be difficult to tell whether he is truly sleepwalking or is awake and wandering about. If you are unsure, watch what he does: sleepwalkers do only very simple things, so if he is carrying out a complex series of actions he is probably not sleepwalking.

Strategy If you are sure your child is asleep during his nocturnal wanderings, it is important not to try to wake him. Instead, lead him gently back to bed, tuck him in and say your special night-time phrase. Although sleepwalking can be spooky to watch, your child will not intentionally harm himself. However, he may trip over objects or fall down steps, so it is important to make sure his room is safe and the stairs are blocked.

Above If your child is a sleepwalker it is important to block the stairs so that he can't fall down them.

special
situations

5

- Lone parents

- Twins (or more)

- Children with special needs

Lone parents

If you are a lone parent, you will know that your child is no different to any other. It therefore follows that all the sleep advice in this book can be applied just as successfully to your family. The big difference, of course, is that when you decide to tackle your child's established sleep pattern you will be doing it on your own.

Commitment

If you are on your own, you may be more tired than other parents you know. And that's before you even begin sleep training!

Sleep training itself can be tough going in the initial days, even when there are two of you. If you are on your own, it is likely to appear even more difficult. But, as we have already cautioned, the worst thing you can do is to start a sleep programme and then abandon it a few days later: your child will know how long it takes to wear you down and will resist even more determinedly next time.

It is therefore even more important that you are completely committed to your new sleep plan, and are determined to make the necessary short-term investment in order to achieve the long-term goal of unbroken nights.

Left Your own parents may be willing to look after your child so that you can have a rest when you start sleep training.

Right If you care for your child alone, tackling her sleep pattern can seem particularly daunting initially.

Support

It is a good idea to get as much support as possible:

- Maybe you have a friend who would be willing to stay over occasionally to help share the night duty?
- Perhaps your parents would babysit in the afternoon so that you can catch up on some sleep?
- Maybe you know another parent who has been through it before, who could act as a phone buddy to help boost your resolve when you feel as though you are going to give up?

Believe in yourself!

It may appear daunting, but you can do this. And doesn't the prospect of unbroken nights sound fantastic? If it seems overwhelming in the first couple of days, remember that with most of the strategies outlined in this book you should see a considerable improvement within only a few days. Even with the 'gradual withdrawal' approach (see pages 50–51), it should take only a few weeks.

'I used to have to lie down with Ella to get her to sleep. I tried tackling it a couple of times, but found it very traumatic and gave up. But when Ella was 3 I had really had enough. I was a lot more determined this time and I also had a housemate, which made a huge difference. Being able to talk things through with her and having her emotional support gave me the back-up I needed to see it through.'

Caroline, mother of Ella (5)

Twins (or more)

Twins can be twice as nice and double trouble at the same time – if you have triplets or more, just keep multiplying the equation! The good news is that there is no reason why multiple-birth children cannot sleep soundly.

There are many reasons why twins, triplets or more can take a while to slip into a good sleeping pattern.

- **They are often born prematurely,** which means they require feeding even more often than other newborns.
- **They are more likely to spend time in special-care baby units,** which means they get used to being touched and nursed at frequent intervals.
- **They are more likely to have different carers at night** – even if they are breastfed, your partner may change their nappies because of the difficulties of dealing with two babies at once – and it can take them a while to get used to the different ways in which they are handled.
- **You may find yourself responding more quickly if one baby cries,** from fear that the other(s) will be disturbed.

Encouraging unbroken sleep

Although their sleep may initially be more disturbed than that of other newborns, getting twins (or more) to sleep need not be any more difficult. All the sleep strategies outlined in this book can be applied just as successfully to multiple-birth children.

The one big difference, of course, is that the babies may disturb one another. Most of the time this won't happen – just as siblings of different ages

Left *Sleep training is just as effective with multiple-birth babies as single babies.*

can usually share bedrooms without waking one another. In fact, many babies are comforted by sharing a room. They may even prefer to share a bed when they are very tiny: check with the Foundation for the Study of Infant Death (FSID) or one of the multiple-birth organizations for the latest advice about co-sleeping and cot death.

However, if your children do disturb one another it may be helpful to separate them, particularly until you have established unbroken nights. If you are pushed for space, move one cot onto the landing as a short-term measure, but make absolutely sure that your child is not able to climb out of the cot and fall downstairs.

Getting support

Try to get as much help as possible. There are charities that provide help for new parents, particularly those with two or more babies. The multiple-birth organizations may also be able to put you in touch with a parent who has been through a similar experience – just talking through your situation can be a big help.

Children with special needs

'Special needs' is an umbrella term that encompasses a vast range of needs and abilities, including difficulties in learning and physiological conditions, either singly or in combination with one another.

It is impossible to answer all such diverse requirements here; however, there are a few pointers that will get you started.

1 **Be realistic.** Although most children with special needs have the potential to enjoy an improved sleep pattern, it often takes longer than for their peers without special needs.

2 **Be prepared.** As it is likely to take even more perseverance to encourage a special needs child to sleep better, you will need even greater resolve. If it is appropriate, try to arrange support from friends and family, so that you can pace yourself and have the occasional break.

3 **See the complete picture.** To give your child the best chance of achieving better sleep patterns, it is important that her diverse needs are taken into account. Most sleep training focuses on behavioural and cognitive techniques, but if, for example, she has Downs Syndrome it may be that she has respiratory problems that are interfering with her sleep – for many children with Downs Syndrome, removing their tonsils alleviates

Left *If your child has learning difficulties you may have to persevere for longer before his sleep improves.*

breathing difficulties. (See also the advice on dealing with an asthmatic child, on page 59.) Similarly, it is important to reflect upon the needs of the wider family.

Above *Every child is different. A sleep specialist can help you devise a sleep programme that matches your child's specific needs.*

4 **Mix and match.** Although your child has unique needs that have to be responded to individually, you can adopt some of the basics of sleep training. For example, establishing a consistent routine will help her to understand that certain things happen in a set order at certain times of the day, and sleep is one of these. Similarly, although no one technique may be right for your child, there may be elements you can use from each that will match her needs and help her to sleep better.

5 **Get help.** You don't have to tackle this alone. Your health visitor will be keen to advise you, or you can consult the paediatric department at your local hospital, or visit a specialist sleep clinic. You may also have access to one of the charities that offers sleep counselling, advice and support to families of special-needs children with sleep problems.

Overview

If you have followed the advice in this book, your baby or child should be on the path to establishing unbroken nights. However, there may be times over the following weeks or months when you want to remind yourself of the key steps to successful nights.

Essential facts

1 By 2 months old, almost all babies have the ability to soothe themselves back to sleep when they wake in the night.

2 Nearly all babies are physiologically capable of sleeping through the night by the age of 6 months.

3 Even older children with an established pattern of disturbed nights can be taught to go to sleep on their own, and stay asleep, in a relatively short space of time.

4 Everyone stirs during their sleep – the trick to achieving unbroken nights is to empower your child to move on to the next phase of his sleep cycle on his own.

Getting it right

1 Creating the right atmosphere can help your baby to sleep well at night.

2 Establishing that nights are for sleeping is fundamental to achieving unbroken sleep.

3 A clear bedtime routine is invaluable in settling your child at night.

4 If you want your child to make it through the night without you, it is essential for you to teach him to send himself to sleep. If you comfort him to sleep, as he stirs in the night he will become distressed when he discovers you are no longer there.

5 There are a number of different strategies for teaching your child to settle himself. Choose the one that suits you and your child best.

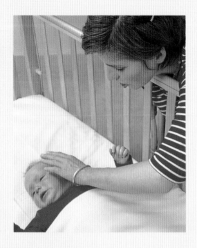

6 Sleep training needs commitment: if you give up after a couple of days, your child will have even more resolve to resist next time.

7 Sleep training can be hard work initially. Be realistic about the challenges ahead of you and try to have as much support as possible in place before you start.

8 Once your child has learned to settle himself, he should naturally progress towards fewer night-time disturbances. However, it is also important that you only respond to him when you are sure he needs you, otherwise you could prevent him from learning to move to the next stage of his sleep cycle on his own.

9 Short-term disruptions and setbacks are unavoidable, but you can take steps to minimize their impact.

10 Rewards can be effective for motivating older children.

And finally ...

If you give up on sleep training, or decide not to start, you could be faced with years of broken nights. But if you follow your chosen strategy properly, you should see positive results within a few days or weeks. Yes, the going may be tough initially, but surely such a short-term investment is worth the long-term prize of sleeping well at night?

Index

Acknowledgements

My thanks go to all the individuals and organizations who have helped in compiling this book, in particular: Jane McIntosh; Joyce Epstein, Foundation for the Study of Infant Death; Jane Ansell, Sleep Scotland; Gingerbread; Serene; Multiple Births Foundation; Twins and Multiple Births Association; National Autistic Society; BLISS; and all the parents who agreed to be questioned about their sleep experiences. And of course my husband and mother, for looking after my own daughters so brilliantly while I was buried in facts about sleep!

Executive Editor: Jane McIntosh
Senior Editor: Clare Churly
Editorial Assistant: Joseph Espiner
Senior Designer: Joanna Bennett
Designer: Bill Mason
Production Controller: Louise Hall
Photography: Peter Pugh-Cook
Stylist: Aruna Mathur

with special thanks to
Babyjunction.co.uk